# UNLEASH YOUR SASS

## IN 21 DAYS, UNLEASH YOUR INNER CONFIDENCE BY REMOVING TOXICITY AND INTRODUCING POSITIVE NEW HABITS

IONA MAY GEDDES

Lady Gaga!
Thank you for being my number 1 role model! I want to be like you when I grow up. Love you x

Unleash Your Sass



First Edition

ISBN (Paperback) 978-1-914447-75-4

ISBN (eBook) 978-1-914447-76-1



This book contains information for entertainment purposes only and should not be used as a substitute for professional medical advice. It is always advisable to consult a medical professional.

Although every effort has been made to ensure the accuracy of the information in this book, no responsibility is assumed for any loss, damage, or disruption caused by errors or omissions, and no liability is assumed for any damages caused by its use.

The views expressed in this book are those of the author alone and do not reflect those of TGH International Ltd.

This book is a work of creative nonfiction, however, certain elements may have been fictionalized in varying degrees, for various purposes to suit the narrative.

Prepared by TGH International Ltd.

www.TGHBooks.com

ACKNOWLEDGMENTS

Thank you all...

I can't thank Sean, and the whole team at The Good House, enough for their constant support through the process of writing this book. I know I wouldn't have finished it without you. Thank you for your mentorship, gentle encouragement and space to feel safe to finish this.

Thank you to every single one of my clients over the last decade who have helped me grow as a coach. It is an honour to support you and every vulnerability has led to the learnings in this book. *It means the world.*

There have been so many coaches, leaders and teachers who have supported my journey over the last decade in my coaching career...

Helen Gillespie and Demelza Feltham, you broadened my spiritual yogic knowledge and you have both helped me more than you know. All of my fellow yogis and yoga teachers who have shared their hearts and souls with me, your love ripples through this book. Every incredible coach and Personal Trainer I worked alongside in my gym years, your wisdom imparted from my million questions a day has given me so much knowledge. Madeleine Ravetta, I think of your teachings in everyday life and with every client I see. Jenny Rose, you taught me the depths of my own femininity. Jill Ritchie, Natalie Gray and Jenny Smith, you have touched my soul and challenged me to look deeper at my connection with myself and Mother Earth.

And last but not least, my friend, soul sister and life mentor Lynette Gray – you are an inspiration and the most joyous soul; the belief you breathe into me every time we meet, gives me so much hope! Without your encouragement, this book would have stayed half written on my laptop!

The support from my friends and family throughout this process has been second to none. A special note to Sarah and Cara who gave me loads of guidance. Your patience with me has been beautiful.

And Kevin, my best friend, living with me isn't an easy task at the best of times but is is even more challenging when I'm doing a project like this. Your constant steadiness, love, care, cups of tea and words of encouragement have helped me more than you will ever know. Thank you.

* * *

Yes, you are scared,
but you are sure to fail if you don't move.
Done is better than perfect.
And imperfect messy action is the most unique beauty of life.

* * *

# CONTENTS

# MY STORY: THE IONA MAY MANIFESTO

Hey, I'm Iona. Welcome to my book. I am the Sass Coach - a Neuro-Linguistic Programming (NLP) Practitioner, life coach and yoga teacher based near Edinburgh, in Scotland. I have worked in the health and wellness sector for 8 years and I have coached hundreds of women to feel happier, healthier and better about themselves.

Similar to so many women, I have previously felt like I was either too much or not enough. Not skinny enough, not beautiful enough, not smart enough. Too loud, too opinionated, too energetic.

This "not enough" story all started with being bullied at school and it grew throughout my life until I learnt the tools (detailed in this book) to begin healing myself and, in turn, support hundreds of women in overcoming their own self-esteem and health issues. I have used this toolkit to become the confident woman I am today and I am here to support you to find your own confidence... to *UNLEASH YOUR SASS.*

I grew up in the '90s on a farm in the middle of nowhere in north-east Scotland, as part of a big family (I am 1 of 5 siblings) which has significantly shaped who I am as person today. I grew up during a time that media was consistent in everyone's lives and the fascination of women's size and weight was a huge part of this media (and sadly still is). I was influenced heavily by popstars and R&B singers who had beautifully sculpted bodies, yet were still labelled by tabloids as "fat".

*If they are fat, then what does that make me in my teenage doughy physique?!*

* * *

Throughout this book you will get to know me as Patient Zero.

Yes, I have the list of qualifications to be a "good coach" but, more importantly, I have lived through experiences where by sharing these parts of my story, I will hope to support your journey. I have lived through disordered eating, body dysmorphia, extreme dieting and over-exercising, which have all led to severe IBS (Irritable Bowel Syndrome). I have tried, succeeded and failed at every fad diet and fitness regime there is.

*I want to empower you to find your own true body confidence by removing toxic obstacles and introducing positive new habits.*

I entered the fitness industry and first studied to become a personal trainer in an attempt to heal my own relationship with food and with my body, realising quickly that there are so many layers to making positive changes in our lives (or not making them). I kept asking *"why do some of my female clients make change so easily and quickly and others don't?"*

I realised this was all a mindset job.

I went on to study NLP (a coaching certification to support the mental wellbeing of my clients) to become a practitioner, originally to heal my own damaged gut and mind as well as create a welcoming environment in a gym for women to feel safe and to flourish. Having coached hundreds of women in weight loss and nutrition over the last ten years, I have gained insight into how we can all improve our health from the inside out, starting with the gut and brain – what we put in our mouths and what we let into our minds.

I am obsessed with the field of nutrition and wellness, and am also a very spiritual individual; I track my menstrual cycle with the moon, I use crystals, I send out intentions to the Universe. I believe strongly in science and strongly in intuition, as well as something bigger than us.

* * *

My aim with this book is to bring knowledge to you, the reader, in the hope that you can take active steps to heal your body, still your mind and improve your life to become your most confident sassiest self!

I hope the words on these pages bring true inner-confidence – *Sass* - into your life.

# A NOTE FROM THE AUTHOR

I understand that many of my learnings in this book have been assisted through having lived in a house with warmth, running water and food in the fridge, not to mention the privilege of having a community around who I could lean on. The privilege of personal development is not available to everyone, however, if and when it is, I encourage the active participation in your own actualisation.

Something to note about this book, is that I have used a lot of the medical terms as wordplay or puns. I am not a doctor or healthcare practitioner so if you feel you need medical assistance in any form – physical or mental - then please speak to the relevant medical professional to seek advice.

I believe self-awareness is a positive thing. The more awareness we can have about ourselves, the more we can change what isn't working, keep what is and share our learnings with each other. I am a strong advocate for taking as much responsibility as we can for our own health and wellbeing through our diet and movement, as well as keeping check of what is going on in our own minds.

It is my mission to support healing and give back to my community. Mostly, this is to support women and those who identify as women; however, this book truly is for anybody as the tools presented in this book are beneficial to *any body*.

After reading this book, if you have changed one habit or shifted one repetitive thought pattern, then you've taken a huge winning step. I ask that you please pass this book onto someone else once you have finished so they can also take this step.

*Iona x*

# INTRODUCTION

In this book I will help you to embrace the natural confidence you were born with, to *UNLEASH YOUR INNER SASS*. Let go of the restrictions that both you and society have put on yourself. Learn how to think, consume and create habits mindfully and with joy. Be at peace with your body, mind and soul.

I want to guide you through your journey to self... Connect to your body. I will share my story through this book, from frantic "ants in my pants" to finding my own peace. I want to share with you how I found all of the tools which have already helped hundreds of women, how they helped me and how you can implement them into your own life. As you learn to love yourself unconditionally, you will find the life you love on the way.

As you read this book, I would recommend journalling as you go. Some of this will emotionally impact you, some will resonate with you, some will make you want to take powerful action. I would also recommend that you start to keep a note of your emotions in relationship to your mind, body, food and movement. Cambridge University Press[1] research shows that journalling for twenty minutes a day can improve memory, boost immunity and decrease depressive symptoms.

Throughout this book there will be an invitation to write and journal. I recommend getting a notebook/journal for this because pen and paper is much more powerful than typing. I also have downloads for this book from the downloads section of my website here:

www.ionamaycoaching.co.uk

A lot of people understand *how* to look after themselves and treat their bodies well. It is putting it into action and then doing this consistently that people struggle with. As women, we have also been conditioned to believe that the norm should be running around looking after other people, leaving no time or energy for ourselves.

A Sage review in 2021[2] on self-help showed that women are more likely to look after their colleagues', family's or friends' needs before their own. As women, we are wired to have a maternal instinct (whether you are a mother or not) as well as societal pressures to conform to this narrative. We exhaust ourselves trying to please other people and keep everyone happy, leaving no time to give back to ourselves. In the end we aren't giving our best to all of the people in our lives. I want to help make a change in this. If, as women, we focus on filling up our own cup first, then we can give so much more energy and compassion to the people and passions that are important to us.

There is also a multitude of issues from the modern day clusterfuck world we live in; not having the tools at hand to deal with all of the daily stresses and notifications, as well as not always having access, or knowledge to access, services that are needed. With this book, my aim is to give you the tools to add to your toolkit that will help you not only survive in life, but really thrive.

By the end of this book, you will have the tools and techniques to instantly drop into your own life and create sustainable change so you feel confident in your body today and for years to come.

1. Baikie, K., & Wilhelm, K. (2005). Emotional and physical health benefits of expressive writing. Advances in Psychiatric Treatment, Cambridge University Press, 11(5), 338-346. doi:10.1192/apt.11.5.338
2. Borghouts, J., Eikey, E., Mark, G., De Leon, C., Schueller, S.M., Schneider, M., Stadnick, N., Zheng, K., Mukamel, D. and Sorkin, D.H., 2021. SAGE Review, Barriers to and facilitators of user engagement with digital mental health interventions: systematic review. Journal of medical Internet research, 23(3), p.e24387.

# HOW TO READ THIS BOOK

This book has 3 sections - My 3-step Sass Method:

Consumption
Mindset
Habits

CONSUMPTION: food and information which mean you can focus on your diet and the information/media you consume.

With reference to Consumption, I am going to focus on two things; food and information. We usually think of Consumption as just the physical things we eat, however, I believe the majority our Consumption comes from information - the media and opinions of others that contribute to the beliefs we have about our bodies, food, diet and everything in between.

Within food, we will explore much more about how and why we eat rather than *what* we eat – from experience I know that all of us know *what* to eat (more green vegetables, lean protein, complex carbohydrates and healthy fats as well as less processed/packaged foods and less alcohol). Most habits surrounding what we eat change naturally when we start to change *how* and *why* we eat.

Under the food element of the Sass Model, we will look at how we label foods, how to eat more mindfully and how to think about what we want to eat more of.

In the information section, we will look at self-reflection of why we eat in certain ways and decide which eating habits we want to stop. We will also look at what information, opinions and media we want to discard and add in, including new affirmations to re-train our brains to speak more kindly to ourselves.

* * *

MINDSET: self-reflection work and spirituality which mean you can create more balance and self-awareness.

In the Mindset chapter we are going to discuss a more holistic approach to your life - this includes a sprinkle of spirituality and self-reflection work. Mindset layers beautifully atop Consumption because it is the deep inner-work that will make the difference between you simply starting a new habit or keeping it up in months, or years, to come.

Under the Mindset chapter you will journal on repetitive thought patterns, cleanse your negative thoughts, administer self-love, fill up your own cup with self-kindness, invest time back into yourself by reading personal development books or investing in yourself and having a dose of meditation to gain more self-awareness and balance.

* * *

HABITS: movement and mindfulness which mean you create more sustainable habits and stay more present for the life you love.

With Habits we are encompassing movement and mindfulness. I believe finding a way to move your body with love and joy is essential in finding deep confidence and trust in your body – finding your Sass. Creating more consciousness and being more present with how we do things gives us more enjoyment in life.

When looking at Habits we will journal/reflect on your Habits and movement, look at what sparks joy, change *one* habit at a time – learn to single-task, move your body with love. I will also recommend for you to try yoga, find exercise you enjoy and reconnect with nature.

# WHY SASS?

# SASS

*SASS* - *noun* [*U*] /sæs/

Talk or behaviour that is rude and shows no respect:

"I don't want to hear any more of your Sass."

*Or so the Cambridge dictionary says...*

* * *

*What I prefer...*

Used in a sentence:

"She steps into the room with effortless sophistication and *SASS*."

# THE SASS MODEL

The Sass Model is the 3-step method I have developed over the years working with clients. I have realised that there are 3 pillars which women need to work on to gain more insight into their own health and body confidence. The 3 pillars:

Consumption, Mindset and Habits.

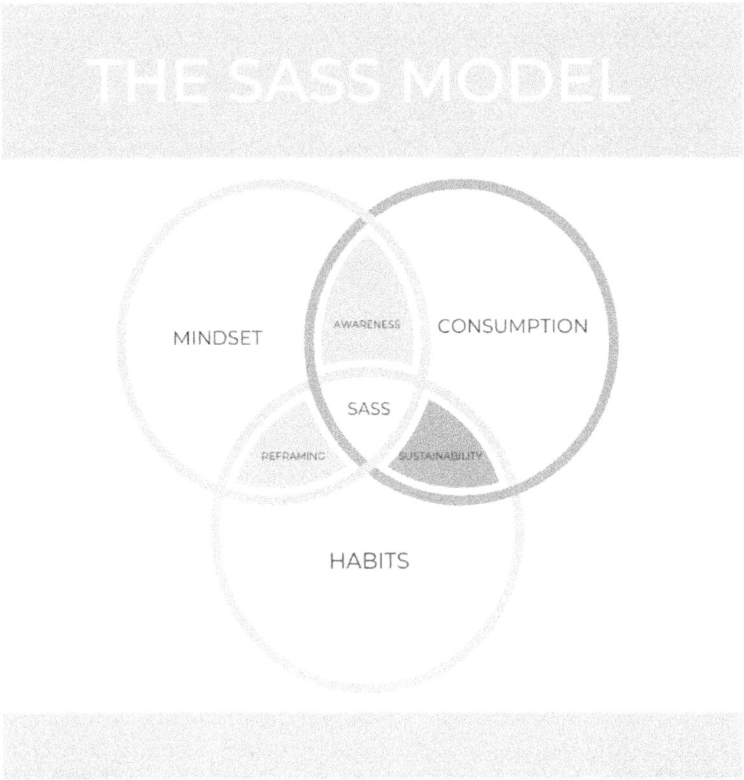


* * *

*The first step on your body confidence*
*journey is self-awareness,*
*learning to trust your intuition.*
*Build trust in yourself and*
*your true inner voice will get louder.*

INTUITION = inner tutor

Overconsumption of:

- Fake news and media
- Fake food
- Fake advice/info

Can lead to:

- Body dysmorphia
- Obsession over body weight
- An unhealthy relationship with food

# WHY SASS?

My wonderful friend inspired the idea when we were spit balling names; she said "you are pretty Sassy".

*I instantly took that as a compliment.*

Sass has connotations of being too loud and too opinionated, of having too much attitude or too much cheekiness, and of stepping out of line. I feel so passionate that these are some of the qualities that women need *way* more of as we continue to break down the patriarchal constructs of which we live in.

Sass, to me, is all about confidence, speaking and living your truth, standing tall and using your voice when it needs to be spoken. My job is to aid women with the tools to re-frame and shift our mindset, empowering ourselves with knowledge and changing our habits to step into that power.

I wish I could bottle up Sass and hand it out to all the women across the planet. Instead, I will let you self-prescribe it in a way that fits your life.

I believe strongly that when women truly love and connect to their bodies, their lives becoming more fulfilling and enjoyable.

Stop wasting time and energy speaking negatively to yourself, worrying about what food you should and shouldn't eat, whether or not your clothes fit right... Instead pour that energy into other areas of your life; your personal development, careers, family, friends, romantic relationships. By doing this, we will all have a fuller life and that confidence will ooze into all areas, pathing the way for more assertive female role models.

GET SASSY AND STAY SASSY.

*What does Sass mean to you?*

# PART I
# CONSUMPTION

# THE BRIDGET JONES BIOPSY 1996+ (A PARODY)

My first memory of overanalysing my body was when I read Bridget Jones' Diary and started weighing myself daily. I was 10 years old.

Let's set the record straight - I love Bridget Jones. I would love to go to the pub with her and set the world to rights. I am against what society made her do. The Bridget Jones movement of the '90s was a cornerstone to the shit show of the fitness industry and media. The movement created a 30–40-year carnage which we are still unpicking from our minds today.

(Current day social media is even worse for comparisonitis and keeping up with the Jones's when it comes to body image – FYI most women's bodies don't look like the ones we see on the internet!)

## WHAT CAN WE LEARN FROM BRIDGE?

- Journalling is a cathartic and beautiful practice
- Singing at the top of your lungs is an energetic release (with or without copious amounts of wine)
- It is not your setbacks that define you, it is your come backs. The bounce back-ability of Bridget Jones is almost unheard of today.
- Don't always listen to your parents. They can sometimes be c**nts.

## LESSONS THAT I LEARNED AS A 10-YEAR-OLD FROM BRIDGE THAT I HAVE NOW UNLEARNED

- Self-deprecation is celebrated, accepting compliments and living by yourself is frowned upon
- Weighing yourself every day is essential for finding love and acceptance
- Binge drinking alcohol and binge eating chocolate are entirely normal and acceptable ways to treat your body

- Hiding your true self from the romantic loves you desire is essential when looking for love
- You need to be saved by a man otherwise your life is worthless

## SOCIAL MEDIA AND COMPARISONITIS

Social media has built very clever algorithms which hook us in. With an ever-diminishing attention span – we are now at a point where the common goldfish has a longer attention span that the average human – companies are competing in classical media as well as social media for space, time and our attention. It's no wonder we are all addicted to our phones! Don't blame yourself for how long you spend sucked into your phone – this is simply a reminder that we have the power to overwrite these algorithms and bring back our own power.

# PATIENT ZERO - ME

## A RECIPE FOR DISASTER

I read Bridget Jones and learned from the age of 10 to weigh myself daily to measure own self worth. Then, as a teenager, I watched R&B videos with women who had rock hard abs and huge boobs (not realising that most of these women had undergone plastic surgery to achieve this).

I started to read magazines full of deathly thin supermodels and actresses who the editors and journalists called "fat".

I disconnected from most girls my own age due to always feeling "different" and a bit of an outcast, then developed an even greater warped reality of what a woman (or girl)'s body should look like.

## WHICH LED TO COMPARISONITIS

I would look in the mirror and wonder where my own rock-hard abs were hiding under the soft marshmallow-like form. I would read up in my favourite magazine about how to "get a 6 pack in 6 weeks". I started to research weight loss diets and then I started to restrict my food intake.

I started getting a bit more attention at school when the fainting started... not realising the damage I was doing to my body.

I decided to become a vegetarian - another great way to gain back control, being able to cook for myself (as well as the ethical/environmental reasons). The obsession with calories developed. I will never forget how many calories are in a banana...

## MEAN GIRLS ARE MOSTLY MEAN TO THEMSELVES

We have all seen the scene in the movie Mean Girls when Lindsay Lohan is at Regina's house for the first time and all the other girls are picking themselves apart; "my nailbeds suck", "my pores are huge".

They turn to her waiting for her to find her own flaws and all she can come up with is "I have bad breath in the morning".

This is because she hadn't been conditioned to focus on her appearance and find the flaws. This is what it is like for us as children. When we are born, we are born pure, non-judgemental. Self-hatred and judging ourselves and others are all learned behaviours.

The beauty of this snippet of the movie is that it shows a teenage girl who hasn't been subjected to the wrath of the media, high school cliques and the general pressures all teens feel.

If we can learn these behaviours and thought patterns to be horrible to ourselves, we can also unlearn them.

## ME AS A 7 YEAR OLD SAYING TO MYSELF...

*My body is amazing*
*Which lets me play and life is fun*
*Every new day brings excitement*
*Meeting new people is a game so find out who they are*
*Everyone loves each other and that includes me.*

And then, to fit in, I had to learn to shrink myself.

Having always had a boldness and outer confidence, being told I was "too much", "too loud" or "full of myself", I felt I had to join in the game of "*who hates their body the most?*"

I repeated these jibes to myself enough times that I started to believe it. Then, I began to build the "I am not enough" story...

*My mission is to support as many women as possible to unlearn these stories and unlearn the beliefs we developed in our younger years.*

# THE FAD DIET DEFICIENCY

## MY PHILOSOPHY OF DIET CULTURE

If you don't already know this, then here is a truth bomb for you...

Most of the mainstream media is endorsed by large corporations who have an agenda. Usually, this an agenda to sell a product to *you*. So, it is beneficial for the media to create a story and a belief within women which gives them a reason to need to buy that thing. They need us to have an unfulfilled need or a pain which needs to be fixed in order to make money.

It has been happening between many large networks and food companies for decades which is why free, life changing, information to make you live better isn't as accessible as it should be. If the mainstream broadcaster (or governments **cough**) can't profit from it, then it won't be promoted mainstream.

A great example of this: we know how damaging refined sugar is for us but it is still in almost every food product on the shelves.

*Knowledge is only power if we use it, so let's empower ourselves.*

# TEENAGE TORMENT

There I was as a 14-year-old girl; riding the hormone waves like every teenager does, mixed in with a generous lathering of bullying, a sprinkle of attention from boys (who were expert bullying makers too – *kids can be so cruel*), powered by a little "too much" Sass and passion to be the centre of attention as a performer. I had always dreamed of being a famous musical theatre actress or singer.

From magazines and media, I read that all the stars were on strict diets, starving themselves or on an intense fitness regime which led to my story, *"I need to become skinnier to be a successful star on the stage"*.

Being told to "suck your belly in" every week at dancing further cemented in my mind that I had a bigger belly than was appropriate for a performer. This reinforced a strong belief of "You are not good enough; you are not enough".

*Does any of this sound familiar?*

One day I decided to start excessively controlling my food intake.

## AGED 12-24, I TRIED THE FOLLOWING FAD DIETS:

- The cereal diet – eat 2 bowls of cereals instead of 2 of your meals and have a third full meal
- Juice cleanse – all in the name, you just drink juiced anything you can find
- Shake diet – similar to cereal but with shakes instead
- High fat diet – avocado for days
- Low carb diet – deprive yourself of all that is good in the world
- Binge and restrict diet – binge for 2 days and be in an extreme calorie deficit for 5 (so spend most of the week starving)
- High calorie/low carb diet – these are similar diets – high protein and dangerously low carb

so you build ketones in your blood, "burn more fat". High protein diets are actually great for most people BUT we need the carbohydrates alongside. I wouldn't recommend doing either of these diets unless recommended for medical reasons (e.g. epilepsy)

- Carb cycling – eat more carbohydrates on training days (this is actually really good for athletes or if you do a sport)
- Classic calorie counting – if done safely and healthily, this can be beneficial but it is just tedious as hell and not a lifestyle most people want to live by

Plus, loads of others I have blocked from my memory...

*And do you want to know the secret I learned?*

All of these diets work. Yup, that's right. You will lose 5 pounds or get skinnier or "get a 6 pack in 90 days" - all of these are possible if you are stubborn enough to ignore your intuition, wants, needs, internal and external cues and blindly follow the diet.

***BUT,*** once the diet or regime is finished, you will end up exactly where you started, if not in a worse position.

No diet or regime ever gave me what I actually wanted – self-acceptance.

They won't make you healthy or happy long term. Whatever you wanted will disappear in the same amount of time you started the diet, if not quicker. We need a more sustainable and holistic solution...

Self-acceptance doesn't mean you feel happy, positive and great 24/7 and your life is perfect. It means you can accept where you are at right now. Love most parts of yourself, accept the other parts and have the tools ready to deal with all things life throws at you!

* * *

*Body confidence does not come*
*from trying to achieve the perfect body,*
*it comes from embracing the one*
*you already have.*

## ENTERING THE VOID A.K.A THE FITNESS INDUSTRY

Entering the world of fitness professionals in my 20s opened up a whole new can of worms. Within 6 months of starting work as a personal trainer and fitness instructor, I had leaned down to the smallest I had been in my whole life.

A cocktail of comparisonitis, feeling the need to be my own walking advert for my business and being one of the few females in a male-dominated environment felt I had something to prove.

I got obsessed, and I loved it. I never got the "6 six pack" but "shredded abs" was always the underlying goal.

*(Please note – if you can stand unassisted then you have a 6-pack underneath whatever fat you have on your belly. Celebrate that 6-pack strength!)*

A plate of food stopped being fun. It was just fuel. I decompartmentalised each food into all of the scientific chemical needs – *is there enough protein here? Just enough calories? The correct type of carbohydrate?*

I didn't even taste my food for about 3 years, but I did not care. Which is why I now still work daily on looking at my food and enjoying it*[1]

I tracked everything that went into my body. Even herbal tea, which is literally the same calorie count as water. I felt the most in control of my body and my life than I had ever been.

When eating out, I checked the menu and picked everything I was going to eat before going. I had my ammo of reasons for not drinking alcohol at the ready whenever a friend would come out with, "Why are you not drinking? Just have one!"

*(Which is entirely unhelpful advice by the way.)*

---

1. More on this in your prescription on Page 45

# PHILOSOPHY OF CALORIE CULTURE

## CALORIES IN VS. OUT SYNDROME (WE ARE STILL IN SURGERY ON THIS ONE)

The Calories In vs. Out Syndrome is an ongoing battle/play of what can go through your head on a daily basis regarding food.

It starts with the want for knowledge. Then you learn a little and it opens up whole new world of unknown. Learning how many calories is in *everything* is usually Stage One. Then you learn what macros are – fats, proteins and carbohydrates. Then how much protein is in everything. You focus on how many calories are in high fat foods and discover that you "should" really only be having 2 teaspoons of cheese instead of the quarter block you enjoy. Then the sugar. Oh me, oh my! The gallons of sugar in everything. Feeling stressed when buying or eating *anything*. Checking the pack of every packet or asking "but what is in it? I need an ingredients list" whenever you eat out or a friend offers something home cooked.

The unhealthy obsession so many of us have with food is tremendous.

As discussed in Pollan's incredible book 'In Defence of Food' we are becoming "orthorexics - people with an unhealthy obsession of healthy eating". We have moved away from eating food for pleasure, socialising, community and much more and instead have developed "nutritionism" - where foods (and non-foods) are simply seen as a mix of the "nutrients we need", instead of foods and raw ingredients being the beautifully complex yet simple entities that they are.

My stance? I think in order to make sustainable change in our lives, we need to educate ourselves about what we are putting in our bodies. Yes, learn about nutrition and why it is important, but also learn to truly enjoy our food and enjoy the eating experience as a whole; the taste, the texture, how it smells, what we can hear and what is happening around us.

However, not everyone will be able to learn this information then let it go and enjoy food for what it is – nutritious-full, a joy in life! There is no "one size fits all" approach, so take all of this information and apply it where it fits into *your* life.

Harvey Levenstein[1] suggested that the excessive choice of food available to Americans, alone, has led to "a vague indifference to food, manifested in a tendency to eat and run rather than to dine and savor".

*When is the last time you took time over a meal? Sitting at a table? Without your phone in your hand?*

* * *

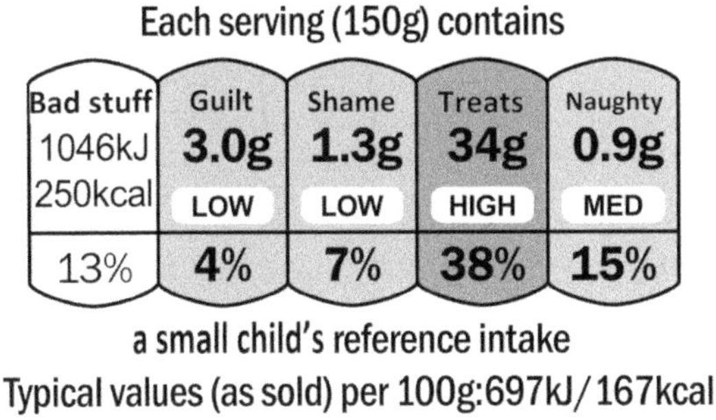


The development of nutritionism brought a promise of better health. However, this isn't conclusive. If anything, our obsession of pulling food apart into individual nutrient components and restricting ourselves has made the western world unhealthier, with the highest rates of heart disease and obesity since the beginning of civilisation[2].

It is time we start bringing back the other important parts of eating – community, cooking, cultivating food, being closer to the process and enjoying the full experience of dining, whether that be alone or with friends and family.

---

1. Pollan, M., 2008. *In defence of food: The myth of nutrition and the pleasures of eating*. Penguin UK.
2. Pollan, M., 2008. *In defence of food: The myth of nutrition and the pleasures of eating*. Penguin UK.

# PRESCRIPTIONS FOR CONSUMPTION

## YOUR RESPONSIBILITY

The recommendations in this guideline represent the view of Iona May Coaching. When exercising your judgement, take into account your own socio-economic situation as well as your own values and beliefs. It is not mandatory to apply these recommendations, however, they may change your life.

## GUIDELINES – CONSCIOUS CONSUMPTION

I believe when it comes to our consumption, there is no "one size fits all" quick fix. Consumption isn't only about what we physically put in our mouths but what we let in. What information, opinions and beliefs we take on build up, to what we consume on a daily and weekly basis which makes up how we think throughout our lives. If we can unpack these, be aware of what we are letting in, create strong boundaries about what we do and don't want to consume, we can start to recreate our own reality of conscious consumption.

*I hope this is Day 1 of your new reality.*

# 7 DAY CONSUMPTION CONTEMPLATION PRESCRIPTION

CONSUMPTION: aim to increase awareness of external factors and build boundaries

## DAY 1: JOURNAL ON YOUR CONSUMPTION STORY

*To me, consumption is more than just what we eat and drink. It is what we let in through our eyes and ears, what we choose to focus on. Whose opinions are we letting in? Which stories we are holding onto? What do we watch on the news or social media? An important question to ask ourselves about all of these actions is, why do we let them in or keep them out?*

Let's rewrite your consumption story... *how do you want it to be?*

Think back over the previous 24 hours and ask yourself:

- Which recurring negative thoughts are you having about your consumption?
- How have you felt after each meal?
- How have you felt after each time you have come off social media/the news/your emails/any media?
- What type of people are you surrounded by? Are these people empowering you or putting you down?
- How have you felt after spending time with colleagues/friends/family?
- What was food like in your house growing up?
- How does that compare to your relationship with food now?
- What is your relationship with your phone (and other devices) like?

Now that we have reflected on what our consumption status is like, we are now going to discard things that aren't serving us to make space for what you *do* want in your life. This works for every area of your life.

*Have you ever noticed that when you do a clear out of your clothes you suddenly find that ideal item you have been searching for?*

Because you physically and energetically made space for it in your house. We are going to do the exact same thing with your consumption!

## DAY 2: REHAUL - UNPROCESS YOUR CONSUMPTION

Reflective Questions:
*What can you get rid of or replace?*
*How can you eliminate unnecessary distractions in your life?*

Reflective Prescription:

Look at the 3 areas of your life where most consumption happens and make a plan to get rid of those that aren't serving you. Pick *one* of these areas today to implement and schedule time in your diary to do the other two.

FOOD – Which foods are not nourishing me? Which do I not enjoy? Which foods leave me feeling bloated or sick afterwards? Go to your kitchen and take out items you don't want to keep. Donate them or offer them to someone who will enjoy/use them.

INFORMATION - Which social media, news or information outlets aren't serving me? Who can I unfollow, delete, hide or block today to create more space?

OPINION CONSUMPTION - Which friends or family opinions aren't serving me? How can I create stronger boundaries to not let these opinions affect me? How can I have conversations with these people to strengthen our relationship and my own?

**LIFE HACK** Boundaries

Boundaries are borders or restrictions to put upon yourself, your actions and other people to protect yourself. This could be at work, with colleagues or with the time you spend doing work, or they could be how you spend time with family. They could be what you do and do not eat or drink. They can cover any area of your life that you want to feel supported or safer in. You can put these in place at any point. They may need a conversation with other people.

For example, if you find you are working more hours than you need to or taking work home with you and it is bleeding into or affecting your home life, then you may decide to create boundaries that say you will turn your laptop off at 5pm or leave the office at this time. To be held accountable, it may be useful to have this conversation with your manager/boss and potentially also your family so they can pull you up on it if you don't stick to it. When having conversations with people about implementing these boundaries, it can be really important to express how *you* feel about what is currently happening and why is it is important to *you* to make the change.

*Where can you create stronger boundaries in your life?*

## DAY 3: FROM LACK TO ABUNDANCE – WHAT DO YOU WANT MORE OF?

Arm yourself with an abundance of knowledge.

What do *you* want to fill your mind and body with? Nutritious foods? Inspiring role models? Supportive friends and family? Uplifting language?

FOOD – Which foods are nourishing me? Which do I enjoy? Which foods leave me feeling satisfied? Which foods did I used to eat and now want to eat more of? Write a list of items you want to add in, especially those with fruit and veggies, incorporate them into your week.

INFORMATION - Which social media, news or information outlets do I want more of? Which kind of people do I want to follow/read more about? Start following accounts who talk about body positivity and educate you. (See my notes at the end of this book for some of my favourite inspiring body confidence and health leaders.*)

OPINION CONSUMPTION - Which friends or family leave me feeling amazing and light me up? Which friends or family opinions aren't serving me? How can I create stronger boundaries to not let these opinions affect me? How can I have conversations with these people to strengthen our relationship?

## DAY 4 - FOOD LABELS – GOOD/BAD/NUTRITIOUS

These labels that we create, or are taught, culminate in the guilt and shame that surrounds diet culture. Over the next 7 days, you are going to unpick these labels and reapply new ones or remove them altogether.

Use the journalling cues below to empower yourself and decide how you want to label them going forwards. Removing words like "bad", "unhealthy" and phrases like "I have been good so..." or "I have been naughty so..."

These are phrases that lead to binge and restriction cycles of diets which are mentally and physically unhealthy, as well as unsustainable.

Michael Pollan[1] discusses the research that shows that a lot of nutrients, when extracted from or added into foods for their known "health benefits", do not in fact give the same benefit as that nutrient as part of a whole food. e.g. extracting omega 3 from an egg and adding it to a food to "fortify it" doesn't have the same effect on the body as eating an egg.

*How do you label foods? Good/bad? Healthy/unhealthy?*

*Which foods do you label good? And which bad?*

If this activity feels challenging, then bring it back to the simple facts and guidelines:

- More vegetables (especially green ones) are always going to support every health goal you have, as well as take you back to basics with food.

- Add in regular protein and carbohydrates as close to the source as possible (e.g. bread with as few ingredients as possible, rice eaten as a whole food) and fats in the most unprocessed form you can find them (flaxseed, nuts, pulses, avocados are all great).
- Processed foods with more than 5 ingredients want to be kept to a minimum – they don't need to be labelled "bad" or "naughty". Looking instead at where these can be swapped out for a whole food replacement where possible.

## DAY 5 - AFFIRMATIONS ON CONSUMPTION

We all use affirmations all day, every day, mainly unconsciously. These are the words and phrases we use to talk to ourselves. They may be mostly positive but as humans we are wired to focus on the negative thoughts when they arise.

The aim of this prescription is to bring our focus back to the positive and resourceful thoughts.

. . .

Your Prescription:

Pick 3 of these to work with. Reword them so they feel right for you. You can say these in your head or out loud, make them the lock screen on your phone, write them on post it notes in your bathroom or rewrite them daily. Make sure you read or write them every day for 7 days and notice how things start to shift.

Before you pick 3, ask yourself:

*What do I want MORE of?*

Pick 3 consumption affirmations:

"I make nourishing food choices daily"
"I am what I eat, and I eat well"
"I am cultivating a deep relationship with my food"
"I can have both (e.g. I am learning to love my body AND improve my health)"
"I am committed to constantly growing"
"I nourish my mind and body daily"
"I enjoy my food"
"I only take in what serves me"
"All foods I chose to eat are nourishing my soul"

## DAY 6: MINDFUL MEALS

When is the last time you ate something without having a screen in front of you (including your phone)? If it was a long time ago, this is normal.

When is the last time you had a day go by without a screen in front of you at all? If you can't remember then this is also normal.

*Normal is not always optimal for our health.*

We all have a circadian rhythm in every cell in our body and the light from screens (as well as many other factors) can knock these rhythms off causing hormonal imbalance, poor sleep, excess stress, anxiety and much more.

Less screen time will always equal more connection. Connection is important to us as humans. We are social creatures and we seek out connection; it supports our mental and physical health as well as unpins why we do a lot of what we do in our relationships and, more importantly, with ourselves. We seek connection eating, sleeping, socialising and taking conscious rest, which many of us struggle to do.

Looking at your food while eating without the distraction of a screen means you will:

- Enjoy and appreciate the food more
- Eat less
- Digest better - the signal from your eyes helps increase digestion

***N.B.*** *You are legally required to take a lunch break (in the UK a least). So take one.*

Your mindful meal prescription:

STEP 1. Schedule in at least 1 meal every day to be eaten at a table. Without screens or distractions. Where possible, do this for every meal of your day.

STEP 2. Reflect on these meals for 1 minute after you finish eating: Did I enjoy and appreciate this food more? Have I eaten more manageable portions? How does the rest of my body feel after eating? Is my digestion better? Am I feeling fuller for longer? What are my snacking habits like?

Repeat every day for 7 days.

## DAY 7 - REFLECTION

Schedule a self-check-up/check-in once a week on a day and time you know you can fully connect back to yourself for 5 minutes. Look back over your week and ask:

- What went well?
- What did I enjoy consuming the most this week?
- What can I consume more of next week?
- What didn't I enjoy or what can I delegate, cut out completely or replace with something else?
- Am I still on the path I want to go on?
- How do I feel?
- How have I nourished my mind, body and soul this week?
- When was the last time I truly enjoyed something and how can I bring it back?
- What can I see myself still doing in a year?

*How do these answers align with your dream goal?*

## Your Dream Goal–Future Visioning Exercise:

Find a quiet space you can sit for 5 minutes. Bring a notepad and pen. Close your eyes and take 5 deep breaths in through your nose and out through your mouth.

Ask yourself the following questions and then journal your responses:

- If there were no barriers, what would you love your body to feel like?
- If you were in the ideal health, shape and fitness what would you see, hear and feel?
- Think of a person who you aspire to be like in terms of health and body confidence... How do they act? What do they eat? What do they do with their days?
- In what ways do you want to do more of these actions?

---

1. Pollan, M., 2008. *In defence of food: The myth of nutrition and the pleasures of eating*. Penguin UK.

# PART II
# MINDSET

# MINDSET MEDICINE - A CASE STUDY

***WARNING!*** Failure to cultivate your Mindset will lead to:

- The Loneliness Infection
- "Social akathisia" – a.k.a "ants in your pants"/busyness for the sake for busyness
- The corporate jungle fever

Failure to cultivate your mindset can lead to low self-esteem, low mood and a high chance of body dysmorphia/imposter syndrome.

In the Mindset chapter we are going to discuss a more holistic approach to your life. This includes a sprinkle of spirituality and self-reflection work.

## NOBODY LIKES ME AND I DON'T BELONG. HOW THE INTERNAL STORY DEVELOPED...

Most of our values, core beliefs and identities are built in our first 7 years of life. It is very interesting to look at your life in patterns of 7 years.

## A TIMELINE
# MY MILESTONES

HERE ARE SOME OF THE PATTERNS THAT HAPPENED IN MY LIFE – TRY THIS EXERCISE YOURSELF AND NOTICE YOUR OWN MILESTONES:

### 1990 - 0 YEARS
Born, happy family life in the countryside in Scotland with 2 older siblings

### 1997 - 7 YEARS
Turn 7, start to become aware of bullies, not fitting in at school. Love performing. Now 2 younger siblings

### 2001 - 11 YEARS
Start to form integral friendships at summer camp. Read Bridget Jones - started weighing myself.

### 2002 - 12 YEARS
Realise my parents marriage isn't "normal". That they might split in the future. Strong want to protect younger siblings from this.

### 2008 - 18 YEARS
Parents divorced and left family home, left school, moved abroad alone for the first time, grandfather and good friend's mum passed away, first big heart break

### 2009 - 19 YEARS
Started uni. Found my sanctuary in the gym and started excessively exercising and dieting, became the lightest and thinnest I have ever been.

### 2010 - 20 YEARS
Got a scholarship to go China for the summer - travelled furthest from home alone. Struggled with food while travelling. Felt "fat" the whole trip

### 2011 - 21 YEARS
Started my first "adult" long distance relationship. Put more pressure on myself to look good all the time. Diagnosis of "probably IBS"

### 2014 - 24 YEARS
Graduated, got my first adult job, moved cities, travelled alone in China again, started my first "side gig" and building my confidence as an entrepreneur, trained to be a PT. Started healing my IBS.

### 2015 - 25 YEARS
Moved cities, become fully self employed for the first time. Become stronger, heavier and the leanest I have been as an advert for my business.

### 2018 - 28 YEARS
Completed my yoga teacher training. Ended first long term relationship, started therapy. Started truly loving and accepting my body. Life changing trip to Nepal on female empowerment. Started to find my female friends tribe.

### 2022 - 32 YEARS
The journey to self-love continues, so happy you are here for the ride...

# PATIENT ZERO: THE LONELINESS INFECTION

The recipe of a young Sassy school girl:

- A bundle of vibrant ginger hair (everyone else was blonde or brunette)
- Early need for a bra and sanitary products
- Learning what stretch marks were aged 9
- Constantly dancing/singing/performing in some way (a.k.a. being a show off)
- Being excessively honest with people

This recipe led to intermittent bullying and feelings of isolation (none of the above characteristics have changed, and I survived, so...)

Throughout my whole life, I always felt like I didn't belong and was "different". Even as an "adult" in corporate jobs I never had the energy for the bitching or gossip, I just wanted to do my job and go home. In friendship groups I could never be bothered spending time with people who were emotionally draining, so I have ended up with a very eclectic group of friends (who I care for deeply).

However, this can cause feelings of isolation.

Most people want you to get sucked into the negativity and gossip so that *you* belong and feel safe. Crab mentality.

Like a pot of boiling crabs, if a crab tries to escape then the rest of the crabs will pull it back in so it stays with the crowd, even when the crowd are on fire... *sound familiar?*

> "In a gradually boiling bathtub you would be dead before you knew it." – Margaret Atwood, *The Handmaid's Tale*

***WARNING!*** The loneliness infection can lead to side effects of:

- Non-deservedness
- Low self-esteem
- Negative self-talk
- Warped idea of self
- Victimhood and pushing people away

The prescription... *A DOSE OF SASS!*

# LONELINESS VS. SOLITUDE

## THE SASS PHILOSOPHY

As I grew up, I started to realise most people feel lonely and like they don't belong. Yet, the truth is that we do belong. We all belong somewhere and we find our people bang on time. I found most of my "tribe" in my mid-twenties, but some people meet theirs aged 12... it's just luck of the draw.

We are constantly sold the idea that being alone is a bad thing; get your life partner, get married, or you are a failure; have a big friendship group and post all your happy clappy photos on social media or your life is a waste; have children and fill your time looking after them or you have not contributed.

This loneliness epidemic has been exacerbated by the Covid-19 pandemic and lockdown measures. Being forced to stay in one place meant so many people either got divorced/moved out or bought a dog/had a baby/got married.

Being alone doesn't need to feel lonely (always) and doesn't mean you don't belong and aren't good enough.

This feeling of being alone, lack of community and lack of connection makes us feel the need to fill *all* of our time with stuff, with doing. This has led to a pressure to fit into societal norms, which means so many women are pushing themselves to adhere to unattainable societal beauty standards which are played out to us by the media, and now social media. Which leads us to be adults addicted to the *doing,* rather than being.

Even when relaxing, we are *doing* – binge watching television, binge eating to fill the void of silence. Alone with our own thoughts. The not-wanting to sit with uncomfortable feelings. Filling the void of silence and "nothingness" with excessive doing - eating for boredom and over-exercising because we are conditioned not to rest.

*Why not take a teaspoon of solitude, intentional aloneness?*

## WHY SHOULD WE REST? AND HOW DO WE REST?

We should actively rest during the day outside of sleep. Yes, getting good sleep is vital; 7-9 hours is healthy for an adult – if you aren't getting this then seek medical support as a lack of sleep affects every system in the body and can create serious and long-term trauma to your body.

> "The shorter your sleep, the shorter your life." - Matthew Walker, *Why We Sleep*

Step 1: look at improving your sleep schedule if possible. Outside of this, active conscious rest (while being awake) is incredibly nourishing for every system in the body. Active conscious rest could include meditation, listening to a body scan or yoga nidra, reading a book, getting out into nature, writing a joy list, journalling, painting or many other creative activities.

A study by Elsevier found that meditating every day for 8 weeks significantly reduced inflammation in the body caused by stress. Other benefits include controlled anxiety and anxious thoughts, enhanced self-awareness, lengthened attention span, increased focus and productivity. It may also reduce age-related memory loss and improve sleep, amongst many other positive things.

# ANTS IN MY PANTS

## BUSYNESS FOR THE SAKE OF BUSYNESS

**TRUTH BOMB** Rest is productive.

*Read that again...*

In order to balance the 2 energies that we all have – the doing energy and the being energy – we need to have both in our lives. We need to create white space or silences to give our minds and bodies time to grow, repair, learn and process the busyness of life. Sleep is an important part of this, but active conscious rest while we are awake is just as important and can sometimes be more nourishing. Active conscious rest could be journalling, reading, meditating, sitting with a cup of tea, painting, yin or restorative yoga or any activities that makes you feel relaxed or in a flow state.

## DIAGNOSIS – "SOCIAL" AKATHISIA

The word *"Akathisia"* is derived from the Greek language and means "unable to sit". (A medical condition similar to feeling ants in your pants)

Social Akathisia can manifest as:

- That feeling that you have forgotten to do something, so checking every app in your phone until you forget that you forgot what you forgot because you get distracted by highly filtered women's faces and figures, feel shit about your "imperfect body" then go in the loop to search again for the thing you hadn't forgotten in the first place... (like a goldfish)
- An ongoing feeling that you aren't good enough, doing enough, being enough
- Poor mental health, feeling depressed or feeling anxious, which can lead to clinical depression or anxiety
- IBS (Irritable Bowel Syndrome)

- Chronic tiredness or fatigue
- Lack of motivation
- *Really* not wanting to get out of bed

Patient Zero regularly struggled to sit still through an episode of something on television (let alone a whole film!) without the feeling of needing to be doing something at the same time.

Distraction activities could be:

- Doing accounts
- Mending a jumper
- Creating social media content
- Scrolling through hundreds of random peoples' photos on social media to attempt to scratch the itch
- Writing a to-do list
- *Anything* to stop you from slowing right down and just watching television or chilling out

I always thought (and still do) that watching most television is a waste of time. A waste of the precious finite time on this planet. Time that could be spent outside, creating, making or building something.

# YIN AND YANG

As adults, we need to learn to balance our doing vs. being energy (or masculine vs. feminine or Yin vs. Yang). Contrary to popular belief, we do not need to be "doing" more. Most of us need to learn to "be" more. *We* are all addicted to doing doing doing, rather than being. We write to-do lists as long as our arm, knowing full well we will never complete them.

Is this from fear or failure? That we won't get "it" all done before we die. Fear of success? That once we have done our tasks we aren't allowed to sit and enjoy some relaxation time.

If no one has told you this before, then you have permission from me to rest. No, I don't mean go to sleep in your bed at night. That is sleep. I mean active, conscious, regular rest.

Our subconscious brains get very busy when we take rest. They get busy processing information, figuring out that work problem you just couldn't figure out. Why do you think the best ideas come to you when you are walking the dog, drying your hair or having a shower? Because these are times you can't be on your phone or looking at a screen, giving your brain time to take a breather.

Society's story is that we *need* to be constantly busy or productive to be "successful" or happy. It is a lie. Although some people still believe it.

Remember those bullies from primary school? Yup, they are still floating around. They obviously haven't read and taken their prescription of this book yet (haha) because they landed up in your office as a 20 something year old...

## MASCULINE AND FEMININE ENERGY

Regardless of which gender we identify as, we all have a mix of masculine and feminine energy. Being male doesn't necessarily mean you express a lot of masculine energy and being female doesn't mean you have 100% feminine energy.

I, personally, hold quite the contrary; I am female and I have always expressed and lived with a lot of masculine energy. e.g. I like to be busy and be doing a lot, I like to "get on with things" and not wait around.

Masculine energy can also be described as Yang or doing energy. Feminine energy is also known as Yin or being energy. *We all need both.*

"It is our light, not our darkness, that most frightens us,
Our deepest fear is not that we are inadequate,
Our deepest fear is that we are powerful beyond
measure" – Marianne Williamson

# THE CORPORATE JUNGLE - FOLLOWING THE CROWD

Corporate jungle is a term used to describe how the internal dynamics of corporates work and how a person must be on the right side of the power centre if they want to get ahead.

***WARNING!*** Corporate jungle disorder is highly contagious when working in an infected area. Be sure to protect yourself by adhering to your prescriptions in chapter 3. Especially days 2 and 3 where you find habits which spark joy and work on changing one positive habit at a time.

When catching corporate jungle disorder, one may experience the following symptoms:

- Weight and body fat gain due to poor work life balance and excessive alcohol consumption
- Warped personal identity; say/do things that aren't true to personal value and belief systems in order to get a promotion
- Prioritise work tasks over time with loved ones
- "Forget" to take holidays
- Poor sleep due to stress and working hours
- Lack of social life except with those whose job you may pursue
- Becoming a lion/bully; e.g., micro manage team/colleagues
- Be aggressive towards other human beings over small decisions
- Copying eating, drinking and drugs habits of colleagues e.g., living off of chip rolls, energy drinks, alcohol and drugs, while forgetting what a vegetable is
- Have an affair with another member of staff
- You may also fantasise about throwing yourself down the stairs in order to break a bone to get a few days out and recover from the disorder
- Chronic backache from sitting for 8-9 hours a day staring at a screen

# SURVIVOR PATIENT "Y" – JIM A.K.A THE ENERGY DRINK GUY

## DIAGNOSIS – CORPORATE JUNGLE DISORDER

Jim (with no finger nails from excessive nibbling, nursing a daily hangover) was disgusted and curious in equal parts at the different vegetables I introduced him to while eating my "rabbit food" lunch at my desk.

"What is that?"

"That is a carrot Jim, it comes out of the ground."

He looked dumb founded as he looked from the carrot to his bright orange energy drink and continued sloshing it back to his hearts content.

Having worked in many infected areas I feel the need to ask, do we "need" to drink a gallon of wine at the weekend to get over the horrible week we just had? Are we just ignoring the issues really at stake just to fit in when we know we have an epidemic on our hands?

Yes, the systemic issues of patriarchal micromanagement within almost every large corporation need to be dismantled. While we work on that in the background, have a seat in the waiting area and I will get your prescription ready for you....

*....a sprinkle of Sass!*

* * *

Imagine having the confidence to speak your truth, live your truth and step into your power? Imagine having the confidence so say, do and be what you really wanted? To quit the job you hate and go for the career you really want. To get that gym membership and start nourishing your body. To wear "that dress" you bought years ago but never had the confidence to wear.

* * *

*Try not to be too busy*
*making a life, that you forget to*
*live your life.*

# PRESCRIPTIONS FOR MINDSET

## YOUR RESPONSIBILITY

The recommendations in this guideline represent the view of Iona May Coaching. When exercising your judgement, take into account your own socio-economic situation as well as your own values and beliefs. It is not mandatory to apply these recommendations, however, they may change your life.

## GUIDELINES – MINDSET

I believe when it comes to our Mindset and mental health there is no "one size fits all" quick fix. The first step is to increase self-awareness and turn down the volume of unhelpful thoughts, then start to increase self-love by feeding our minds with kinder thoughts. We can also focus on investing time and energy on filling up our own cups, making time for mindful practices like meditation to give our minds time to decompress from the busy and full lives we all live. Our brains are powerful machines, gently nudging them daily to remind them we are a team is a great practice to get into. Ease into these practices.

# 7 DAY MINDSET CONTEMPLATION PRESCRIPTION

MINDSET: aim to increase awareness of thoughts on our own body

## DAY 1: SELF-AWARENESS PRESCRIPTION

*The first step to changing your life for the better, is to create awareness of where you are now. To take a huge leap across a stream you want to, make sure your footing is strong and you know where you are jumping from, to ensure you land safely and can continue well.*

The self-awareness prescription is to be administered either first thing in the morning or before bed. Use a pen and paper for the best results.

Some identities and beliefs we have developed through life will always be there, whilst some we can work through and fully release. How can we catch the ones which are sticking around quicker and reframe them to become more resourceful in our current state?

The practice here is to notice them, catch yourself and ask, "Is this true?"

Think back over the previous 24 hours, ask yourself these questions and journal on them:

- Which recurring negative thoughts are you having about your body and health?
- What is stopping you from having what you want right now?
- What are these negative thoughts you are having?
- Who told you them? Was it a teacher, parent, a partner, society, the media, yourself?
- Where did this come from?
- If it is something negative about your body, ask yourself "Would I say this to a friend or a stranger?" (*If the answer is "no", then why would you say it to yourself?*)
- Your mind and body are your home, why let aggressive and negative thoughts in?

- What need are you fulfilling by repeating these thoughts and patterns?

You may need to repeat this prescription multiple times in your life to peel away extra layers of your onion.

## Being Resourceful in Your Current State

You are maybe thinking "I feel depressed and all I want to do is cry, how is that action resourceful?"

In fact, it is.

The more self-awareness you develop, the more you can learn your own true needs and act upon them. Feeling sadness or any "negative" emotion is an essential part of the human experience and leaning into what you require to soothe that feeling is vital in building trust in yourself. Sometimes the action you need is to lie on your sofa or bed and cry, journal, moan and let out anything that needs to come out. Other times, when feeling low you may need to go out for a walk or go to the gym to raise your serotonin levels and give yourself a natural energy boost.

All of these reactions are helping you become resourceful in your current state.

## DAY 2: THOUGHT CLEANSE

Peel the onion.

I believe, in life, we are born as pure beings with only love and compassion for ourselves and everyone around. We aren't born hating our bodies, being racists or assuming things or people are dangerous – that is all learned behaviour.

For the first 7 years of life, we build our beliefs and values depending on what happens to us, then we strengthen those beliefs through life experiences and our own interpretation of those experiences. We place meaning on everything we do and that happens to us.

Our work in life is to unpeel these layers, to strip back to the core of who we really are, were and always have been underneath the conditioning of society. This is where we truly know ourselves and can find peace.

You may need to repeat this cleanse multiple times to release these matted beliefs from your subconscious and write the letter to many people, or even yourself, to start to release.

One book I love is titled 'The Chimp Paradox'. It speaks about your inner chimp or inner voice – we all have one.

The theory is that you can name your "chimp", then communicate with it rather than let it run loose in your mind. Mine is called Susan. Susan is a bitch. On a regular basis I need to say "Shut up Susan, you are not needed here".

I have been doing this work for over a decade and these voices still come up. These practices will give you the tools to react in a better way to what life throughs at you.

*Thought Cleanse*

Which thoughts need disposing of?

Find a safe space for this exercise where you won't be disturbed.

Write a letter to whoever you feel implemented those thoughts/beliefs from Day 1. Let everything out. Be angry, sad... feel the feelings you need to, to let it out. Write anything that has been left unsaid. No one will ever see this paper so your words are safe on the page.

Once you are finished, sit with any emotion you need to let out. Fully let it all out. Burn or rip up the paper. And dispose of it safely.

Dosage: repeat as necessary.

## DAY 3: ADMINISTER SELF-LOVE

Until now, we have mainly been focussing on the negative. In order for an infected cut to heal, we sometimes need to unpick it and clean it out which can be painful. Then we can look at a dressing it and protecting it. Here is the start of your dressing.

Write a love letter to your body. No, this isn't a joke. List all the parts of your body you struggle with and start to find tangible ways you can love them. Think about what different parts of your body do for you on a daily basis; they help you breathe, pump blood around, eyes that let you see this beautiful world etc.

Once the letter is written, sign "With love from *Insert your name*"

Read it to yourself every day in the mirror. Ideally you want to be naked. Read it out aloud for the best results. This may be painful to begin with but will give you lifelong Sass if you continue the full prescription.

Repeat the prescription if your internal chimp/Susan starts being infected with bitch syndrome in the future and needs cleaned out.

. . .

Example of a love letter to your body:

*Dear Body,*

*I know I haven't spoken to you kindly in the past. I am sorry for calling you fat and useless and all the other horrible names. Here are some things I love about you... I love my belly and all it does for me; it helps me bend and flex, digest my food, protect and cushion my organs, helps me stay healthy.* (etc.)

*Love from Iona May X*

## DAY 4: AFFIRMATIONS AND HOW YOU WANT TO TALK TO YOURSELF

Identify someone who has the body confidence and health goals that you want.

*How do you think they talk to themselves?*

Start with one of the phrases you have written from Day 1 (negative phrases about yourself), then create a neutral or positive opposite phrase to say to yourself instead. It needs to be neutral or positive and in the first person singular so starting with "I am..."

Make sure you remove any negative words like "not", "don't", "can't" or "less/lose".

Please see an example below:

- Old negative thought pattern: "I am fat and useless"
- New neutral affirmation: "I accept my body and have purpose" *or* "I am learning and I am becoming..." options
- New positive affirmation: "I love all parts of my body and I am a powerful woman!"

Use the version that feels most right for you now and upgrade to a higher level and more powerful phrase when that starts to feel easy.

Dosage: take 2-3 times a day on top of a habit you already do, e.g. every time you get dressed or get into the shower, brush your teeth or get into bed.

Refill and reassess these once a month.

## DAY 5: PERSONAL DEVELOPMENT BOOKS - INVEST TIME BACK INTO LOVING YOU

Self-care isn't always bubble baths, it is sometimes about investing time and resources into yourself.

Check in with the health list.

STEP 1. Use the list on the next page to look at all areas of your body confidence and health goals and give yourself a rating from 1-10 in each area: 1 being terrible and 10 being amazing. Whichever part you score the lowest on, is the area to focus on.

STEP 2. Go to my recommended reading list at the end of this book to find a book on this subject area *or* go to an internet search engine and find a book or audiobook to fit this topic (it may be the one you are reading right now).

STEP 3. Follow all the exercises in the book you find. Absorbing new information and reflecting on yourself is really useful. Putting these learnings into action will create huge waves in your life and the results are likely to be longer lasting when you take action while doing the work on yourself.

Physical health markers:

- Cardio vascular fitness/resting heart rate
- Body fat *or* muscle mass percentage
- How clothes fit/waist to hip ratio
- Cholesterol, blood sugar, hormone levels (thyroid/insulin)
- Hydration status
- Injury status and risk
- Sleep levels
- Stress levels

Mental markers:

- How do you feel in certain outfits?
- How do you feel naked?
- How do you feel with food and diet?
- Relationship with alcohol/other substances (sugar, drugs, cigarettes)
- Relationship with exercise

## DAY 6: ONE DROP OF MINDFULNESS AND A DAILY DOSE OF MEDITATION

Conscious solitude is something we need to relearn and administer daily.

Alongside affirmations, meditation and mindfulness practices will support you in your body confidence journey. Over time you will cultivate deeper compassion for yourself. Every time you notice your thoughts running into a negative space where you are talking to yourself negatively or telling yourself "you need to do more", or if you just feel generally overwhelmed, take 2 minutes to do the meditation exercise below.

Meditation practice is just that, a practice. Which we need to cultivate daily. No, you don't need to sit cross legged under a tree with your eyes closed (although go for it if that is your bag). All a meditation practice is, is giving ourselves time to process our thoughts and unpack what is going on in our minds, bodies and souls (if you want to get deep with it).

Next time you notice your thoughts running too fast or going into a negative space, then catch them. Take 2 minutes to focus on your breathe and come back to the present moment. This is building on your mindfulness and meditation practice.

**Top tips on meditating:**

If you are new to meditating and aren't sure where to start, downloading an app or watching a meditation video on the internet can be a great place to start. Some of the apps I have used in the past are 'Calm', 'Insight Timer' and 'Headspace'. There are loads of other great ones too.

I recommend to start with a 2–5-minute meditation. Repeat this every day for seven days and see how you feel (have your journal to hand after your meditation). Once this feels comfortable, then add time on until you find a length that suits you or, more importantly, that you can fit into your routine *regularly*.

Your meditation practice is the same as working a muscle. It is more beneficial to practice meditating for 2 minutes every day for a month than 14 minutes once a week for a month. Your mind, like a muscle, needs regular attention to get into the groove of doing it.

***N.B.*** Meditation for most people will be frustrating, boring and messy a lot of the time. The rumour that you find peace instantly is a lie. My yogi guru, Helen Gillespie, told me that meditating for her is like a filing cabinet for her thoughts; sometimes in meditation, *all* of your thoughts come out of the filing cabinet and scatter everywhere, but by the end you have put some thoughts away and, most importantly, the one you need to focus on today has shown itself.

Meditation gives us time and space to organise our thoughts.

* * *

HO'OPONOPONO PRAYER/MANTRA: I'm sorry, please forgive me, thank you, I love you.

Ho'oponopono prayer is a Hawaiian prayer and mantra that has come back to me many times in my life. You can find a recording of this online easily. Alternatively, simply saying the words above to yourself as you breath in and out is perfect.

Breathing practise:

STEP 1. Find some calming music, or silence if that feels better, and a quiet spot to sit upright - this can be on a chair, on the floor or maybe on your bed. Meditation can be used to help you relax before bed, however, I recommend starting your practise upright so that you gain the benefits for restful stillness without being asleep.

STEP 2. Sit with your feet flat on the floor if you are in a chair, or however is comfortable if you are seated, so that your back is straight and your neck is long. This position will help you get as much breath in as possible and give you the best experience.

STEP 3. Take your time to inhale as deep as you can, then open your mouth and let all the air out.

STEP 4. Breathe in for 3 counts. Hold your breath at the top for 4 counts. Exhale for 5 counts.

STEP 5. Repeat Step 4, 10 times.

STEP 6. Gently open your eyes, have a stretch then go on with your day or journal on anything that comes up.

Your daily dose of meditation and breathing practice – the 3, 4, 5 breathe – is to be taken at any time of day, once a day for a week. Continue prescription if symptoms have subsided.

## DAY 7 - SUNDAY CHECK-IN AND REFLECTION

Like any prescription, the dosage, dispense rate, recipe, number of refills and how it is taken needs to be personal to the patient.

Here is the fun part... reflect on the last 6 days of prescriptions to find which unleashes your personal Sass the best.

Take this prescription with a cup of tea/coffee/water and lemon and reflect on these:

- What worked well this week?
- What did I enjoy the most?
- What did I enjoy the least? And what is important about that?
- What would be beneficial to have more of?
- What is working?
- What can you see yourself still doing in a year?
- How do these answers align with your dream goal?

Use these answers plus your prescription download from www.ionamaycoaching.co.uk/downloads

# PART III
# HABITS

# HEALTHY HABITS

***WARNING!*** If you are not cultivating your Sass, structure and schedule, then you're following the structures and norms of society which cultivate your sedation, stagnation and stupefaction.

*What are Habits?*

You have probably heard a lot about the word Habit, so much so, it is a word you are sick of hearing. However, Habits make up every decision we make, meaning they are a huge part of how our life runs; whether we are happy or not, feel fulfilled or not, love our bodies or not plus so much more.

"You do not ride to the level of your goals. You fall to the level of your systems" – James Clear, *Atomic Habits*

James talks about why having a foundation of strong Habits, which you can either withhold or still make happen on your worst days where appropriate, are what will bring you to where you want to be.

In this chapter we are going to talk about Habits in relation to movement and mindfulness.

I believe movement is a very important Habit we must make for other all good health and, in my opinion, is an essential step in the Sass Model.

I happen to be a huge advocate of yoga (I am a yoga teacher) and will be sharing yoga practices and philosophy as I feel they weave into building confidence beautifully. You may, of course, pick your movement but this book will specifically discuss yoga.

Let's talk about the other overused word of the 21st Century – mindfulness.

*Why this is important and why it will help you?*

I want us all to spend less time with Habits like lying on the sofa and binging television or mindlessly scrolling on social media. (The average person in the UK spends 2.5 hours using social media daily – that is 56 days a *year!*)[1]

Imagine how different your life would look, and feel, if you changed some of those habits to become more present and in the moment with yourself and your loved ones.

"Every action you take is a vote for the type of person you wish to become. No single instance will transform your beliefs, but as the votes build up, so does the evidence of your new identity." - James Clear

---

1. Twenge, J.M., Joiner, T.E., Rogers, M.L. and Martin, G.N., 2018. Increases in depressive symptoms, suicide-related outcomes, and suicide rates among US adolescents after 2010 and links to increased new media screen time. Clinical Psychological Science, 6(1), pp.3-17.

# BODY DYSMORPHIA CONTAMINATION – THE EXERCISE QUESTION

## CASE STUDY "X" - ME

The operation: plonk a highly vivacious, performing girl (yeah, me) into a school which wants young people to perform physically in a structured way i.e. team sports. Being developed for ballet but not for football (or any team sport for that matter) led to the evolution of self-loathing. Constantly being picked last in sports due to having zero skills or coordination in this area, deepened the wound of "nobody likes me" syndrome .

*I still can't throw or catch well and I am doing alright so if this is/was you, you will also be fine.*

This experience led to thoughts and affirmations of "I wish I could be like everybody else" and "I just want to be normal".

As we all now know, 1. There is no such thing as normal and 2. Everybody else is already taken. The world needs only one Iona May.

The next threat to a Sassy adulthood was poor self-esteem which cascaded through teen and young adult years. I hit my 18$^{th}$ year with a cocktail of:

- Parents' divorce
- Grandpa and glue of the family passing
- Leaving school
- Moving out of the family home and into a suitcase
- Death of a close friend's mum
- Working 3 jobs in the summer holidays to save up to travel across Europe and Asia to escape it all
- Spending most of that year in a bikini or comparing myself to much prettier, skinnier (in my eyes) private school girls on my ski season
- Being dumped by my first "real love"
- Then dumped again a year later by my "real love" (yeah, the other one...)

# THE MOVEMENT MELTDOWN

## THE SASS PHILOSOPHY

Movement and exercise in modern day society is a mess. My school story is not uncommon and the increased use of devices makes high school children even more inactive. We have taught young people the same lesson as adults; you are either good at team sports a.k.a. you are sporty. Or you are lazy.

*Like prescribed drugs, prescribed exercise is a short-term fix to a long-term problem.*

As we have evolved as humans, something has gone wrong with our movement patterns. Chronic back pain and hating our ever-expanding bellies have both been normalised as a "part of life". Obesity is at at an all-time high - over 60% of adults in the UK are overweight or obese[1].

Here is a truth bomb for you: we were not built to sit at desks for 8 hours a day. We were built to move, walk run and explore. As teenagers, we continue to build an identity of ourselves as "a sporty person" or just... not.

Movement, exercise and life, for that matter, aren't so binary. There is a type of movement to suit every lifestyle that can be enjoyable now and for a long time to come. I believe one of my missions in this life is to help you find that happy place in moving that body of yours!

---

1. Briggs, A.D., Mytton, O.T., Kehlbacher, A., Tiffin, R., Rayner, M. and Scarborough, P., 2013. Overall and income specific effect on prevalence of overweight and obesity of 20% sugar sweetened drink tax in UK: econometric and comparative risk assessment modelling study. *Bmj*, 347.

# EXERCISE AKATHISIA

Exercise akathisia is similar to social akathisia but with an inability to take rest days, or hours, except when sleeping.

I got addicted to exercise at when I started university. It was like therapy to me.

I developed what I describe as exercise akathisia through a combination of:

- Believing that something external and aesthetic needed to be fixed after a double helping of being dumped at a fairly young age.
- Never feeling skinny or light enough, regardless of the excessive calorie deficit from a

cereal diet I was on (just don't do it). Little did I know that feeling "good enough" was an inside job.
- Feeling like I was finally good at a "sport" when I was able to gym 2-3 times all day 7 days of the week.
- Realising the two things I could control in life were what I ate and how I moved.

I lost a significant amount of weight when I moved to Edinburgh for University; I was the thinnest I have ever been and I felt like I was finally "healthy". My Personal Trainer even told me that my friends were jealous when they had commented on my skinny/gaunt look. Little did I know that I had fallen into disordered eating and had severe body dysmorphia. And my friends were trying to help me out of it.

**Note: there isn't a right or wrong way to support a friend who you can see is struggling, just let them know you are there for them. There are loads of resources online to support you with this like BEAT, NHS and Mind.*

Then the physical pain arrived in the form of IBS. Side effects of disordered eating can lead to damaged organs and, in this case, a damaged gut.

My symptoms included:

- Severe cramping
- Constipation
- Diarrhoea
- Extreme bloating
- Fatigue
- Brain fog
- Nausea

After many tests at the doctors came back clear, I was diagnosed with "probably IBS" and given a leaflet about the FODMAP diet. Not to knock the NHS and incredible health support we have here in the UK, but I found this unhelpful so I decided to take my health into my own hands.

Then came the journey of self-healing. I didn't want others to go through what I went through, so I decided to learn how to heal my gut and then pass this information on. That was 10 years ago. I wanted to start looking at my whole health picture, not just at the aesthetic side. I realised the fitness industry was a mess and I wanted to help fix it, so I read every book and journal article I could find about IBS and, later, trained as a personal trainer specialising in nutrition. Through this process, I began unpicking and unpacking my own mind, body and spirit.

Throughout my life, I have always been an outwardly confident person but I was ready to peel back a layer of the onion and find my true inner confidence.

And so I did.

*Then came the Sass Method.*

# WHY PRESCRIBED "ONE SIZE FITS ALL" EXERCISE DOESN'T WORK

The fitness industry is changing for the better, however, there is still a *huge* onus and pressure on all of us to exercise in a structured way. Yes, I agree that every human can benefit from weight or resistance training in some form. However, you don't need to be in a gym in skintight lycra to do so.

One thing I will call out right away about the fitness industry is that women especially have a completely unrealistic and unnaturally picture of "beauty" to live up to. I know many women who are body builders or compete in a sport so they are the leanest and fittest people in our population. They are doing regular exercise for their job and in incredible shape and have had boob jobs or other work done because sometimes when your body fat percentage goes below a certain level to live lean, a lot of this reduced fat will leave your breast tissue. Yes, there are a handful of women who have huge boobs and flat tone stomachs due to their genetics plus hard work – I cheer you all on.

*However,* a lot of the bodies we see with this composition have had surgery. (Also cheering on all the women who choose to do this). All I want to say, is that you do not need to get surgery to gain self-worth. You *are* beautiful right now and, yes, you can still work towards your health goals in a sustainable and healthy way, but you don't need breast implants (or any implants, tucks or procedures) to be beautiful and feel worthy. I know a lot of women who have had procedures done and felt the same about their bodies. Most of this work is internal. Work on your mindset towards your body for a sustained amount of time before making a decision to go under the knife.

I feel the fitness industry's responsibility is to let women know what is real and what is filter. Social media now showing us when something is a filter is a good start; we can unscramble our idea of these ridiculous beauty standards we are attempting to live up to.

PT's and coaches, let's be open with our clients about work we have had done, therapy we have had and be transparent role models so our clients know what is realistic for them to aspire to.

* * *

*Building your body confidence*
*is an inside job.*

# HEALING MY RELATIONSHIP WITH MOVEMENT

## AN INJECTION OF YOGA

During my quest of fixing the fitness industry (a tall task, I know) I fell upon a community yoga class by a friend (and now personal yogi guru and teacher) Helen Gillespie. I fell in love with the physical aspect straight away - the idea of stretching and strengthening muscles while coming into control of the breath at the same time... *genius!*

Then came Svasana (Sanskrit word for corpse pose) - still my favourite part of class. This is where you lie in stillness, either in meditation or focussing your mind on your breath, at the end of the physical practice. This usually turns into a semi-nap for me!

The first Svasana is always memorable - I felt a rush of energy, long before I had learned about chakras and meridians (further information below). You take time to notice how your body really feels when I stop. Stop moving, doing, to-do listing. Just stop. It feels abnormal and uncomfortable to just lay there "doing nothing". During my first Svasana, I think it was the first time I had properly relaxed outside sleep in years. Then there was a release and it felt amazing. A glow... a sweaty post exercise glow and also energetic glow! That was me hooked.

***N.B**. I will be forever grateful to Helen for answering all of my questions and, eventually, becoming the teacher that taught me to teach yoga. My Scottish yoga guru. Thanks Hel.*

## CHAKRAS AND MERIDIANS CRASH COURSE

In ancient medicine there are 7 chakras, "wheels" or energy centres across the human body which sit within different areas of the body along your spine and represent different issues or areas of your life to work on. The aim is to keep all 7 chakras open to allow energy to flow through you with ease.

Meridians are a similar concept in Chinese medicine. We have 361 energetic pathways (or meridians) through our bodies which allow energy to flow. This is the basis of acupuncture and reflexology practices.

# THE WOKE YOGI OUTBREAK

***WARNING!*** Once you start the prescription of regular yoga, you will develop an uncontrollable tic of telling everyone you meet "You need to go to yoga - it fixes everything and it will change your life."

Yogic philosophy is now a way of life for me. Yoga actually has 8 branches. All of these branches are written in Sanskrit (ancient language). Only 1 of these branches/limbs is the physical practice, or Asana.

Most yoga teachers will tell you they practice physical yoga every day. They might, but I definitely don't. However, I do practice at least one of the branches shown below, every day. The main one being Ahimsa – one of the "Yamas" or disciplines/guidelines in yogic philosophy.

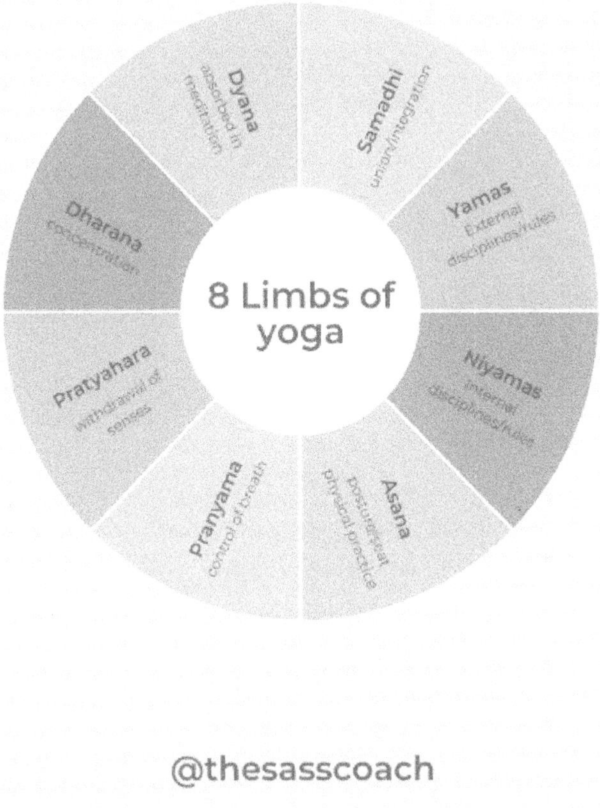
8 Limbs of yoga
Samadhi
union/integration
Yamas
External disciplines/rules
Niyamas
Internal disciplines/rules
Asana
posture/seat physical practice
Pranyama
control of breath
Pratyahara
withdrawal of senses
Dharana
concentration
Dyana
absorbed in meditation
@thesasscoach

**5 YAMAS**

1. Ahimsa (non-violence)
2. Satya (truth)
3. Asteya (non-stealing)
4. Brachmacharya (connection to self)
5. Aparigraha (non-attachment)

**5 NIYAMAS**

1. Saucha (cleanliness)
2. Santosha (contentment)
3. Tapas (self-discipline)
4. Svadhyaya (self-reflection)
5. Ishvarapranidhana (surrendering to a higher power

Ahimsa is the first Yama or "way of life" which means non-violence. I take this compassion.

This, to me, means giving self-compassion first and then compassion to others. When we look after ourselves and listen to our own needs, we are able to serve others with more energy. If our thoughts and actions are violent towards others, it usually means we are being harmful towards ourselves first and this interaction is simply a reflection of our inner worlds.

One way to work with this energy is our conscious and unconscious affirmations.

Take one limb of yoga into your movement daily - some days will be to rest and lie on the sofa, some days will be doing a HIIT workout.

I believe Ahimsa and self-compassion start with self-awareness. *How can you know what you what to change if you don't take stock first?*

# PRESCRIPTIONS FOR HABITS

## YOUR RESPONSIBILITY

The recommendations in this guideline represent the view of Iona May Coaching. When exercising your judgement, take into account your own socio-economic situation as well as your own values and beliefs. It is not mandatory to apply these recommendations, however, they may change your life.

## GUIDELINES – HEALTHY HABITS

I learned at a very young age that life is short. Don't spend your time and energy with people who pull you down or drain your energy, because this energy draining syndrome is contagious. Create a barrier to protect your own non-infected energy.

Our journey to creating healthy and sustainable habits is a life-long journey. Once we feel like we are settling in and getting to know ourselves, another life event will happen that changes and moulds us into the newer version of ourselves. Here are a couple of tools I have used to help me through life's challenges and used with clients over the years.

This is only the start of the journey. Take some learnings into your life and create more balance for yourself.

# 7 DAY HABIT CONTEMPLATION PRESCRIPTION

HABITS: aim to reflect on our previous Habits towards our health and body confidence and change them

## DAY 1: REFLECTION – SELF-AWARENESS MONDAYS. REFLECT ON HABITS AND MOVEMENT

Let's rewrite your Habits story; how do you want it to be?

Grab a pen and piece of paper. Think back over the previous 24 hours and ask yourself the following questions. Some will land, those that don't, just skip.

- What are your current movement Habits? .g. the scroll hole, sitting a lot
- What are your negative Habits?
- How does doing this negative Habit keep you safe? e.g. scrolling on your phone/apps mindlessly means you don't have to face difficult questions
- What need are you fulfilling by repeating these thoughts and patterns?
- How do you feel about this?
- What was the ethos around exercise and movement Habits in your house growing up?
- How does that compare to your relationship with exercise now?
- Do these Habits align to your goal?

***N.B.*** Use your notebook to journal or go and download your free workbook from my website.

www.ionamaycoaching.co.uk/downloads

## DAY 2: CONDUCT A HABIT REHAUL – WHICH HABITS SPARK JOY?

Movement and Habits are only sustainable if you can see yourself doing them in 1, 5 or 10 years from now. If it is something you see as a quick fix or short-term solution, then it won't last and you will end up back where you are now or worse off. The more you fill your days with joy, the more your life is filled with things you love and, before you know it, you will be living the life of your dreams... *what has changed?* Your attitude towards the activities and the choice of activities.

Recommendation:

STEP 1. Split your page into 2 columns. Brain dump a list of all the Habits you want to stop in one column. Then make a list of all the ways you love to move your body and Habits you want to start in the other column.

STEP 2. Make this into a beautifully written or typed list and stick it up somewhere you can see it every day! (I have mine hanging in my office)

STEP 3. Pick one habit *every* day for a week from the bin list to stop, and pick one of the "love/add in" list to replace it with. If you are tight for time, then schedule them in at the start of your week, share with me on social media and tag me to hold you accountable or, even better, get a friend to do it with you! Bring your kids, your friends, your colleagues, your postman on this journey with you!

STEP 4. Once you have worked through all of your "stop" list (this may take a few weeks) then scribble out the "stop" column and rewrite your "love" list on a fresh piece of paper. Pick one Habit you love every day and do this for *you*!

Use the downloads from www.ionamaycoaching.co.uk/downloads

**Habits to Bin:**

- Scrolling on social media for hours on an evening
- Getting home from work and lying on the sofa until bedtime
- Endlessly snacking through boredom at night
- Worrying about your body
- Over exercising e.g. 5 times a week, or more
- Going to the kitchen for snacks throughout the day when working from home
- Eating through stress
- Saying no to friends who want to meet me for a walk because you are worried about being too unfit to keep up
- Putting off going to the gym

**Habits to Start or Continue:**

- Being outside in nature
- Walking with your bare feet in the sand/water
- Swimming in the sea
- Forest bathing
- Meeting/laughing with friends
- Having a cup of tea in bed with a book or in the garden
- Getting a massage
- Giving and receiving thoughtful gifts
- Having a spa day or at home spa day
- Dancing on your own or out with friends
- Singing along to music, either alone or with friends
- Enjoying eating a brownie or cookie
- Exploring/finding somewhere new
- Planning holidays/adventures
- Climbing mountains
- Getting dressed up
- Organising or decluttering
- Spending time with family
- Having a drink in a fancy glass with big ice
- Drawing/painting
- Going on a solo date every week
- Date night

- Making a den and watching an uplifting film

## DAY 3: SINGLE-TASKING YOUR HABITS WITH BOUNDARIES – CHANGE ONE AT A TIME

Accountability, boundaries and taking things one step at a time are the best ways to create new Habits that will truly last.

Preparation: before you do this exercise, journal or reflect on the following questions:

- Who else needs to know or who may you need support from to change these Habits? e.g. people you live/work with
- How will these new Habits affect your life and *their* life for the better?
- How can you create stronger boundaries so that you can see these through?

Create your *ideal* week using the template from the free downloads section of my website then look at how you can work back and put some of those "ideal tasks" into your upcoming week. Or, delegate tasks which someone could support with. Reflect on this every 2-3 weeks.

Use the downloads from www.ionamaycoaching.co.uk/downloads

## DAY 4 - YOGA ASANA (PHYSICAL/BODY) PRACTICE

As part of the Sass Model and Movement section of this book, we are going to do some basic yoga moves. A critical element of self-care is to create boundaries and time for yourself to create safety and trust in your own body. When I studied my yoga teacher training, I learned yogic philosophy which taught me more about this.

Yoga has helped me, and thousands of other people, reconnect to our bodies. Mind-body connection and connection with our breathing brings us back to the basics of our health and wellbeing. It always brings me a deep feeling of gratitude for all the amazing things my body does for me every day.

Recommendation:

STEP 1. Wear something comfortable - this can be gym clothes, your pjs or anything in between. Lie flat on the floor; if you have a yoga mat then use this, but you don't need one, you just need enough space for the length of your body.

STEP 2. Flow through the moves as the diagram below shows and notice where your mind is during the moves. Aim to inhale when you stand or raise your arms and exhale as you move towards the floor. If your mind wanders, bring it back to focus on your breathing.

STEP 3. Finish either back in your lying position or in a seated position and come back to your meditation or journalling practice. If you struggle to sit still but know you need it, pick your favourite relaxing or chilled song and sit and listen to it while watching a candle flicker.

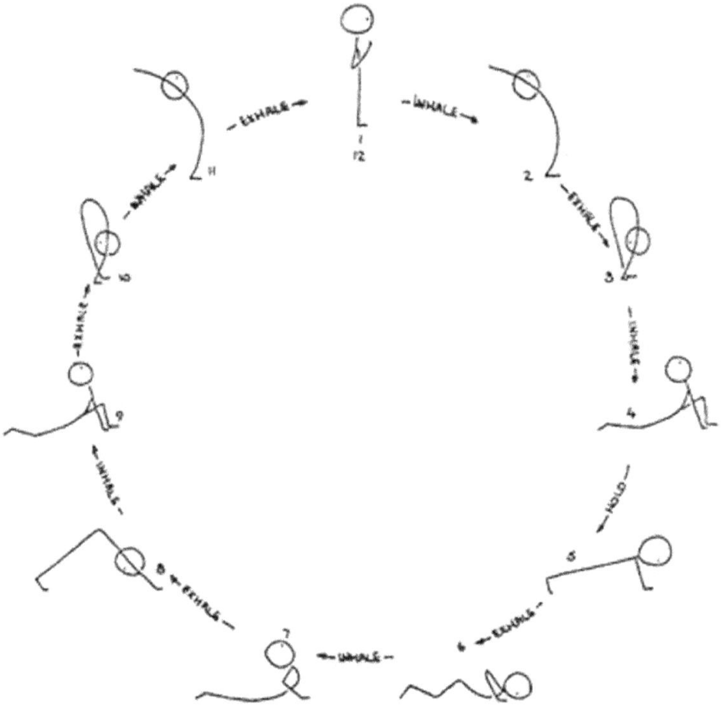

## DAY 5 - BUILD CONFIDENCE MOVING IN YOUR AMAZING BODY

Having spent a decade in the fitness industry, I have been through a personal journey, flipping the idea of why I weight train and exercise on its head. I started out weight training purely for aesthetic reasons and now I train for so many other reasons which come over and above how my body looks.

Weight or resistance training, for me, has been the number one thing to build my confidence in my own body. Showing up for myself consistently at the gym 2-5 days every week, without fail, for the last 8 years has built so much belief in my own staying power.

It also provides the benefits listed below:

- Less liable to injury (for me, my knees hurt less when climbing mountains – a hobby I *love*)
- Increased bone density which decreases the chance of osteoporosis and arthritis in older age
- Improved immune health
- Improved circulation which can, in turn, improve the lymphatic system
- Increases the body in space awareness
- Improved posture and decreased likelihood of back pain
- Improved mental health
- *And* maintained muscle mass which helps to look more toned!

My number 1 top tip to take away from the prescription on Day 5, is to look at the movement or exercise you currently do or want to start doing. Write down all of the benefits this exercise gives, or will give you, *over and above* weight loss, fat loss or any other aesthetic reason. This will give you more staying power on the days you are tired and will bring you more enjoyment for the activity as a whole, meaning it will become a part of your lifestyle and not simply a way to punish yourself.

Add in some weight or resistance training alongside this practice in a gym or at home. This will supplement any other movement or sport you already do *or it* will give you longevity in your health and body for the rest of your life if you don't have another form of movement already.

## DAY 6: RECONNECT TO YOUR BODY AND MOTHER NATURE

"We still do not know one-thousandth of one percent of what nature has revealed to us." - Albert Einstein

Simply being outside can relieve stress and calm the mind because being outside lowers cortisol in the body, as well as reducing blood pressure and heart rate. It strengthens our immunity by increasing the number of white blood cells in our blood, as our immune system is often challenged more when we are outdoors. It sharpens our focus and makes us more alert when we get back to work/life, as well as enhances creativity.

Exercising outdoors can also aid in weight management as we have so many things to look at and think about as a distraction, so we can burn a lot of energy and increase circulation by being out and about. The calming effect of greenery in nature helps improve our long- and short-term memory, as well as improves our vision because the natural light works in harmony with our eyes. Spending regular time outdoors can increase longevity of your life! It's a no brainer really; wherever you can, get outside and get stuck into nature!

Even without all of the science, I have always found getting my trainers or walking shoes on and stepping outside into the fresh air to be very soothing. We often get stuck in our thoughts, busy being busy in life. The trees don't care about the cellulite when you are wearing your shorts. The sky doesn't judge the extra few pounds you have gained. The birds don't mind that you don't have any make up on. The flowers don't see each other as competition, they simply bloom. All they see is your natural beauty.

Finding gratitude for the simple act of breathing in fresh air, acknowledging how amazing our lunges are and our heart is, and remembering how connected we are to nature, always quietens the loud negative voice in my head.

Get outside – *how?*

- Create strong boundaries with your family, friends and coworkers for getting out and about. Even show them the above data to get them involved.
- Schedule in outdoor time and, wherever possible, socialise outside. The last few years have shown us the power of spending time outdoors with loved ones, so let's carry on that trend.
- We all have colleagues who take smoking breaks. Irrespective of your colleagues behaviour, taking breaks is important, so schedule in your fresh air breaks in and find any greenery near your place of work.
- As you walk notice your 5 senses. What can you see? What can you hear? What can you feel? How warm or cold is it? What can you smell? What can you taste? Whichever of your senses feels strongest, tune into it. e.g. if it is your sight, stop by a leaf and really take it in -

look at the detail of the veins, any bumps on the surface. Notice the miracles all around you and within you.

## DAY 7 – CHANGE HABITS

Reflect on the last 6 days of Habits, movement and new activities you have tried. Take some time to journal on these and make a plan for the next 7 days.

- How much have I moved my body this week?
- What movement have I enjoyed the most?
- What is working?
- What is my biggest challenge?
- What do I do to stay focused?
- Are those Habits beneficial for me or are they destroying me?
- What new Habits I must develop to turn things around?
- What can you see yourself still doing in a year's time?

***N.B.*** Use your notebook to journal or go to my website and download your free workbook.

www.ionamaycoaching.co.uk/downloads

# THE NEXT CHAPTER

# UNLEASH YOUR SASS...

I don't want this to be another book that sits on your shelf and gets dusty. I want you to use the prescriptions in this book on a weekly basis in a way that works in your life. I recommend you use and reuse this book.

If you haven't already, go back and schedule all of the prescription exercises into your diary and start implementing them into your life, now. Look back at your journal from Day 1 and notice what has shifted already. Celebrate how far you have come and enjoy the rest of this life-long journey of unleashing your Sass.

I believe true inner confidence or Sass is just another description of inner peace. If we were to go big...

*How do we save the world?* By all gaining inner peace.

*How do we all gain inner peace?* By finding true confidence deep within ourselves. By living our truth.

Have you ever met someone who exudes confidence – not arrogance, simply confidence? They speak with conviction; nothing seems to phase them. They stand tall and you know when they have entered the room even though they haven't said a word. Now that, is what I call Sass.

*How have I developed my own Sass?*

Firstly, my own relationship with consumption has changed a lot over the years. I used to consume food and information unconsciously, not even knowing the damage it was doing, and then I became obsessed with every piece of food that passed my lips and was obsessive about what I did/didn't watch or listen to. Now, I am in a place where I am much more unattached to foods; I listen to my body and eat what I want and feel my body needs at the time. Sometimes that is a fresh salad full of veggies, sometimes it is a salted caramel chocolate brownie... for breakfast.

With my information consumption, I now have stronger boundaries. I don't entertain conversations or relationships which are toxic or draining. I don't watch the news. I don't follow social media accounts that make me feel rubbish about myself. I consciously seek out information and people I find empowering and nourishing.

*I hope you can find the right balance with your own consumption through using the tools and techniques in this book.*

Mindset has been the biggest shift for me. From being incredibly self-critical, feeling lonely and lost a lot of the time (even when surrounded by people) and struggling with my own true self-esteem, I have now moved through a lot of self-reflection work and connected deeper in my spiritual self. This has allowed me to remove feelings of guilt or shame from what I do/don't do. I am still working on finding my own balance between doing and being, but I have so much more self-awareness and seek to soothe my mind whenever I can.

My Habits have changed significantly over the years. I used to do things for all the wrong reasons – because it was what everyone else did, because "that's just what you do" etc. I have come such a long way from having "ants in my pants", unable to relax and sit through a television show without busying myself, to now taking radical responsibility for my health, life and confidence through conscious rest and recovery. I now also truly listen to my body and its needs, move in a way that feels good and take days off when my body needs it.

I hope this is a place that you are working towards or a goal of where you want to be. I know that if you follow the prescriptions in this book, you will be on the right path. Layer by layer, you will peel off the layers of your own "onion" which no longer serve you and unleash that Sass which you now know is already deep inside you, just waiting to come out and shine! I want to help you connect to your inner goddess!

Regardless of what you believe, you are both the descendant and the ancestor of powerful women and, whether you like it or not, you are a magical being... you might just not know it yet.

* * *

Imagine having Sass and confidence in your own body. Wear *that* outfit "you could never pull off". Get naked without a care in the world. Throw on that bikini on holiday and know you are looking great. Imagine not spending another moment of your life worrying that you are "too fat", "too thin" or too much for any outfit/job/event/person. Imagine instead pouring that time and energy into things you really care about – your career, your family, your friends, your hobbies!

Imagine a world of self-loving and confident women, who lift each other up because they are overflowing with energy and passion. I wish I could bottle up Sass and hand it out to all the women across to planet. Instead, I will let you self-prescribe it in a way that fits your life...

* * *

I hope you enjoyed this book. It means the world to me that you are on this journey with me. If you did like it, then share it far and wide - spread that Sass around the world!

# RECOMMENDATIONS AND REFERENCES

## REFERENCES

1. Baikie, K., & Wilhelm, K. (2005). Emotional and physical health benefits of expressive writing. Advances in Psychiatric Treatment, Cambridge University Press, 11(5), 338-346. doi:10.1192/apt.11.5.338
2. Borghouts, J., Eikey, E., Mark, G., De Leon, C., Schueller, S.M., Schneider, M., Stadnick, N., Zheng, K., Mukamel, D. and Sorkin, D.H., 2021. SAGE Review, Barriers to and facilitators of user engagement with digital mental health interventions: systematic review. Journal of medical Internet research, 23(3), p.e24387.
3. Pollan, M., 2008. *In defence of food: The myth of nutrition and the pleasures of eating*. Penguin UK.
4. Walker, M., 2017. Why we sleep: Unlocking the power of sleep and dreams. Simon and Schuster.
5. Twenge, J.M., Joiner, T.E., Rogers, M.L. and Martin, G.N., 2018. Increases in depressive symptoms, suicide-related outcomes, and suicide rates among US adolescents after 2010

and links to increased new media screen time. Clinical Psychological Science, 6(1), pp.3-17.

6. Briggs, A.D., Mytton, O.T., Kehlbacher, A., Tiffin, R., Rayner, M. and Scarborough, P., 2013. Overall and income specific effect on prevalence of overweight and obesity of 20% sugar sweetened drink tax in UK: econometric and comparative risk assessment modelling study. *Bmj*, 347.

RECOMMENDED READING LIST

## Consumption

- In Defence of Food – Michael Pollan
- How Not To Die – Michael Greger MD , Gene Stone
- The 4 Pillar Plan – Dr Rangan Chatterjee
- Ignite the Fire – Jonathan Goodman
- Hunger - Roxane Gay
- Why We Want Eat: Fixing Your Food F*ckedupitude – Krista Scott-Dixon
- The Marshmallow Test – Walter Mischel
- Get Ripper or Die Trying – Paul Hussey

## Mindset

- The Chimp Paradox - Steve Peters
- E2 – Pam Grout
- Notes on a Nervous Planet - Matt Haig
- The Universe Has Your Back – Gabrielle Bernstein
- You Can Heal Your Life - Louise Hay
- Mastering Your Mean Girl - Melissa Ambrosini

- How Emotions Are Made: The Secret Life of the Brain - Lisa Feldman Barrett
- How the Pill Changes Everything: Your Brain on Birth Control - Sarah E Hill
- Girl, Wash Your Face - Rachel Hollis
- You Are a Badass - Jen Sincero
- The Power is Within You - Louise L. Hay
- The Secret – Rhonda Byrne
- Manifest – Roxie Nafousi
- Rewire Your Brain - John B. Arden PhD
- Start with Why - Simon Sineke
- Your Best Year yet – Jinny Ditzler
- Awaken the Giant Within – Tony Robbins
- Good Vibes, Good Life - Vex King
- Untamed - Glennon Doyle
- How to Fail - Elizabeth Day

**Healthy Habits**

- Atomic Habits – James Clear
- The One Thing – Garry Keller
- The 5 Second Rule - Mel Robbins
- Wild Power - Alexandra pope
- Code Red - Lisa lister
- Period Power -
- Gut – Guilia Enders

- The 10X Rule: The Only Difference Between Success and Failure - Grant Cardone
- The Big Leap - Gay Hendricks
- The Power of Habit - Charles Duhigg
- The Miracle Morning – Hal Elrod

## RECOMMENDED PODCASTS

- She Loves Herself - Jill Ritchie
- Happy Place - Fearne Cotton
- Super Soul - Oprah Winfrey
- Everything is figureoutable - Marie Forleo
- Dear Gabby – Gabrielle Bernstein
- The Model Health Show – Shawn Stevenson
- The Menstruality Podcast – Red School
- The Melissa Ambrosini Show – Melissa Ambrosini
- The Food Medic – Dr. Hazel Wallace
- The Rachel Hollis Podcast – Rachel Hollis
- Feel Better Live More – Dr. Rangan Chatterjee
- Dirty Mother Pukka
- The Genius Life
- Barbell Logic
- Mind Pump: Raw Fitness Truth
- 99% Invisible
- Made of Stronger Stuff

Ingram Content Group UK Ltd.
Milton Keynes UK
UKHW020317080623
423046UK00011B/193

9 781914 447754